Bernard Madoff

Materminding a Billion Dollar Fraud

Filiquarian Publishing, LLC.

Bernard Madoff – Masterminding a Billion Dollar Fraud is available for free download at www.biographiq.com/bookd/madoff

Filiquarian Publishing, LLC.

Bernard Madoff

Masterming a Billion Dollar Fraud

Bernard Lawrence "Bernie" Madoff (born April 29, 1938 in New York City to Ralph and Sylvia Madoff) is an American businessman and former chairman of the NASDAQ stock exchange. He founded the Wall Street firm Bernard L. Madoff Investment Securities LLC in 1960 and was its chairman until December 11, 2008, when he was charged with perpetrating what may be the largest investor fraud ever committed by a single person.[1] He is under house arrest until his indictment, expected in mid-February 2009.[2]

On December 10, 2008 Madoff allegedly stated that the asset management arm of his firm was a giant Ponzi scheme--or "one big lie."[3] They then passed this information to authorities.[4][5][6][7][8] The following day, Federal Bureau of Investigation agents arrested Madoff and charged him with one count of securities fraud. Five days after his arrest, Madoff's assets and those of the firm were frozen and a receiver was appointed to handle the case.[9] According to federal charges], Madoff said that his firm has "liabilities of approximately US$50 billion."[5][10][11] Banks from outside the U.S. have announced that they have potentially lost billions in dollars as a result.[12][13] Some investors, journalists and economists have questioned Madoff's statement that he alone is responsible for the large-scale operation, and investigators are looking to determine if there were others involved in the scheme.[14]

Madoff's firm, which is in the process of liquidation, was one of the top market maker businesses on Wall Street (the sixth-largest in 2008),[15] often functioning as a "third-market" provider that bypassed "specialist" firms and directly executed orders over the counter from retail brokers.[16] The firm also encompassed an investment management and advisory division that is now the focus of the fraud investigation.[10]

Madoff was also a prominent philanthropist who served on the boards of nonprofit institutions, many of which entrusted his firm with their endowments.[17][18] The freeze of his and his firm's assets have had effects around the world on businesses and charities, some of which, including the Robert I. Lappin Charitable Foundation, the Picower Foundation, and the JEHT Foundation have been forced to close as a consequence of the fraud.[17][19][20][21]

Personal

Bernard L. Madoff was born in 1938 to Jewish parents Ralph and Sylvia Madoff. He grew up in the Laurelton section of Queens, N.Y. In the 1960s Sylvia's brokerage firm, "Gibraltar Securities", registered in her name with her home address as her place of business,[22] had compliance issues with federal investigators.[23][24]

He graduated from Far Rockaway High School in 1956,[25] attended University of Alabama for one year, then transferred to and graduated from Hofstra University (then Hofstra College) in 1960 with a degree in political science.[26][27] The following year, he attended Brooklyn Law School, but did not continue.

Madoff is married to his high school sweetheart, Ruth Alpern, who has been involved with the firm and in the Madoff Charitable Foundation. [28][29] It has been reported that Mrs. Madoff had reconciled the firm's bank accounts. [30] They have two sons, Mark and Andrew.[31] Andrew, the younger son, was diagnosed with lymphoma. In March, 2003, Andrew began serving on the Board of Directors of Lymphoma Research Foundation, and the Madoff family became major donors, contributing more than $1 million in 2007.[32] Deborah Madoff, Andrew's wife, filed for divorce the day before the scheme collapsed.[33] Andrew, the younger son, was diagnosed with lymphoma. In March 2003, Andrew began serving on the Board of Directors of Lymphoma Research

Foundation, and the Madoff family became major donors, contributing more than $1 million in 2007.[34] Deborah Madoff, Andrew's wife, filed for divorce the day before the scheme collapsed.[35] Mark took his money out of the investment arm to fund a divorce from his first wife in 2000 and both sons used outside investment firms to run their own private philanthropic foundations, but Andrew had millions invested with his father.[36]

Madoff lived in Roslyn, New York in a ranch house through the 1970s[27] and since 1981, has owned an ocean-front residence in Montauk.[37] His primary residence on Manhattan's Upper East Side, is valued at more than $7 million,[38] and he is listed as chairman of the building's co-op board.[39] He also owns a home in France[40] and a $9.3 million mansion in Palm Beach, Florida,[41] where he is a member of the Palm Beach Country Club. Madoff owns a 55-foot (17 m) fishing boat named Bull,[39] which is docked in the French Riviera.[42]

Career

In 1960, Madoff started his firm as a penny stock trader with $5,000 (about $35,000 in 2008 dollars), earned from working as a lifeguard and sprinkler installer.[43][44] His fledgling business began to grow with the assistance of his father-in-law, accountant Saul Alpern, who referred a circle of friends and their families, some who wintered in North Miami Beach others, who summered at the Sunny

Oaks Hotel in New York's Catskill Mountains.[45] Initially, the firm made markets (quoted bid and ask prices) via the National Quotation Bureau's Pink Sheets. In order to compete with firms that were members of the New York Stock Exchange trading on the stock exchange's floor, his firm began using innovative computer information technology to disseminate its quotes.[46] After a trial run, the technology the firm helped develop became the NASDAQ.[47] At one point, Madoff Securities was the largest buying- and-selling "market maker" at the NASDAQ.[46]

He was active in the National Association of Securities Dealers (NASD), a self-regulatory securities industry organization. His firm was one of the five most active in the development of the NASDAQ. He has served as the Chairman of the Board of Directors and on the Board of Governors of the NASD.[48]

Several family members worked for him. His younger brother, Peter, was Senior Managing Director and Chief Compliance Officer,[46] and Peter's daughter, Shana, was the compliance attorney. Madoff's sons, Mark and Andrew, worked in the trading section,[46] along with Charles Weiner, Madoff's nephew.[18] Andrew Madoff had invested his own money in his father's fund, but Mark stopped about eight years ago.[49]

The Madoff government investigation believes the fraud in the investment management division and advisory division may have begun in the 1970s.[50] In the 1980s, Madoff's market-maker division traded up to five percent of the total made on the New York Stock Exchange.[46] Madoff was "the first prominent practitioner"[51] who paid a broker to execute a customer's order through his brokerage, called a "legal kickback",[52] which gave Madoff the reputation of being the largest dealer in NYSE-listed stocks in the U.S., trading about 15% of transaction volume.[53] Academics have questioned the ethics of these payments.[54][55] Madoff has argued that these payments did not alter the price that the customer received.[56] He viewed the payments as a normal business practice: "If your girlfriend goes to buy stockings at a supermarket, the racks that display those stockings are usually paid for by the company that manufactured the stockings. Order flow is an issue that attracted a lot of attention but is grossly overrated."[56]

By the 2000 Internet boom, Madoff Securities' reputation was one of the top traders of securities in the nation, holding approximately $300 million in assets.[46] The business was located on floors 17, 18, and 19 of the Lipstick Building, 18 and 19 housing administration and stock-trading, and the investment management division, referred to as the "hedge fund", on 17. The latter employed a staff of approximately 24.[57] Madoff ran a branch office in London separate from Madoff Securities which employed 28, handling investments for his family of approximately £80 million.[58] Two remote cameras installed in the London office permitted Madoff to monitor events from New York.[42]

Methods of Operation, Accusations, and Case

Investment Strategy

Madoff's sales pitch was an investment strategy consisting of purchasing blue-chip stocks and then, taking options contracts on them.[59] It would appear Madoff chose a failed trading strategy, and to compensate for the losses, he began a client-based Ponzi scheme[49] since at least, 2005.[60] In 2001, Barron's Magazine described his strategy from his hedge fund "Offering Memorandum":[61] "Typically, a position will consist of the ownership of 30–35 S&P 100 stocks, most correlated to that index, the sale of out-of-the-money 'calls' on the index and the purchase of out-of-the-money 'puts' on the index. The sale of the 'calls' is designed to increase the rate of return, while allowing upward movement of the stock portfolio to the strike price of the 'calls'. The 'puts', funded in large part by the sales of the 'calls', limit the portfolio's downside." In 1992, Madoff explained his strategy to the The Wall Street Journal: In the 1970s, he had placed invested funds in "convertible arbitrage positions in large-cap stocks, with promised investment returns of 18% to 20%,"[59] and in 1982, he began using futures contracts on the stock index, and then, placed "puts" on futures during the 1987 stock market crash.[59]

A few analysts performing due diligence were unable to replicate the Madoff fund's past returns using historic price data for U.S. stocks and options on the indexes.[62][63] It is doubtful Madoff made any or all of the required trades this strategy dictates, because purported trade volumes appear to far exceed the listed derivative open interest.[64] Rather, Barron's raised the possibility that Madoff's returns were most likely due to front running his firm's brokerage clients.

Three steps of the split-strike or collar trade are: 1) buy a stock at price, "X" —, say 100; 2) selling a call option with a strike price, "Y" —, say 120 —, which is above "X"; and 3) purchase a put option with a strike price, "Z" —, say 80 —, which is below "X". If the stock price is 125, which is above "Y" at expiration, the stock will be called away, and the investor receives "Y" (120) for the stock. If the price is 70, which is below "Z" at expiration, the "put" can be exercised and "Z" (80) is received in cash. This caps the maximum gain (until the options expire) at the Y minus X (120 − 100 = 20), and the maximum loss at the X minus Z, (100 − 80 = 20). Depending on the cost of purchasing the "put" (say 4% annualized), the premium received to write the "call", (say 3%) and the dividends from the stock holdings, (say 2%), the options transactions can generate positive or negative cash-flow. To create an effective collar for a long-term stock holding, the option contracts should be rolled into contracts farther out, prior to expiration.

Lawrence R. Velvel, dean of the Massachusetts School of Law,[65] and Madoff investor, explains Madoff's strategy according to Frank DiPascali, Madoff's assistant: Madoff was engaging in the "split-strike conversion" strategy. He bought for one's account a "basket" of stocks in the S&P 100. To guard against losses, he simultaneously bought options, or "puts, allowing him to sell the stocks -- to "put" them to someone, if they went down instead of up. To pay the purchased "puts", he sold other options, named "calls". After small gains, that allowed the buyer of the option, to "call" the shares from Madoff, he could make small profits on the numerous trades when shares rose. This was done by guarding against losses via "puts", while offsetting the price of the "puts", by selling "calls", which limited the gains from each set of transactions, and by repeating the process with highly active trading during the course of a year. "Madoff was swinging for singles, not homers", said DiPascali, while he guarded against big losses from downturns. Over the course of a year, the small profits would mount up, about one or one-and-one-half percent, and would exceed any small losses when stocks went down and then, would be "put" to buyers.[66] This method appeared to be a "credible" way to obtain financial gains.

Rival fund managers were unable to replicate the same returns, using the strategies from Madoff's quarterly reports.[67]

5% Rule

Madoff masterminded a scheme, typical of a Ponzi scheme in its structure, except it differed in its pace and its marketing. The true secret to Madoff's success was his lifetime involvement with non-profit charities, and the tax law knowledge he gleaned from that experience over many decades.[68] Charitable foundations became the basis, as well as the collateral damage of his surreptitious strategy. He exploited his own social networks, and over time, received implicit entry into new venues to promote himself and his company among a largely upper-class clientele. He invested their significant funds consisting of educational foundations and social charities, as directed by them. The slow pace and ongoing cliquish "insider" word-of-mouth marketing enabled the deception to survive for several decades. It grew beyond the expectations of a common Ponzi. All was quite successful, the perfect crime, until it appears that the autumn market meltdown of 2008 and extraordinary demands for cash by other investors in early December overwhelmed his well-oiled system.[69][70][71]

Ultimately, charities and foundations which invested with Madoff lost millions, in what has been characterized as a form of affinity fraud. Mitchell Zuckoff, professor of journalism at Boston University, author of Ponzi's Scheme: The True Story of a Financial Legend, explained "the 5% payout rule," a federal law requiring foundations to pay out 5% of their funds each year. As long as a foundation's principal earns 5% a year - not always possible in a given year, but a reasonable goal over time - a foundation endures, and so does its sponsor. Madoff knew the federal law well. Zuckoff noted, "For every $1 billion in foundation investment, Madoff was effectively on the hook for about $50 million in withdrawals a year. If he was not making real investments, at that rate the principal would last 20 years. By targeting charities, Madoff could avoid the threat of sudden or unexpected withdrawals." Zuckoff suggests that years ago, Madoff "solved the two interlocking puzzles that usually prevent Ponzi schemes from becoming perpetual money machines: sustaining growth, while maintaining stability."[69]

Sales Methods

Rather than offer (suspiciously) high returns to all comers, Madoff offered modest but steady returns to an exclusive clientele, produced in both up and down markets. The investment method was marketed as "too complicated for outsiders to understand". He was "cryptic" about the firm's business. He ran a secretive business, and kept his financial statements under lock and key, not unlike the Treasury Secretary or the Chairman of Federal Reserve.[72] The New York Post reported that Madoff "worked the so-called 'Jewish circuit' of well-heeled Jews he met at country clubs on Long Island and in Palm Beach".[73] The New York Times reported that Madoff courted many prominent Jewish executives and organizations among those investing in his funds: Jeffrey Katzenberg, Eliot Spitzer, Yeshiva University, the Elie Wiesel Foundation, and charities set up by the publisher Mortimer Zuckerman and Hollywood film director Steven Spielberg. One of the most prominent promoters was J. Ezra Merkin, whose fund Ascot Partners steered $1.8 billion towards Madoff's firm.[67] A scheme that targets members of a particular religious or ethnic community is a type of affinity fraud, and a Newsweek article identified Madoff's scheme as "an affinity Ponzi" and called the man behind it "the most sophisticated and charming huckster of all time."[74]

Madoff was a "master marketer",[27] and his fund was also considered exclusive, as he was initially giving the appearance of being very selective of which investors to take on, giving the appearance of a "velvet rope".[67][27] For the most part, he refused to meet directly with investors, which gave him an "Oz" aura and increased the allure of the investment.[42] Some Madoff investors were wary of removing their money from his fund, in case they could not get it back in later.[15] One New York real estate investor said she "literally begged" Madoff to take her money, and he refused.[58]

Fairfield Greenwich Group, based in Greenwich, Connecticut, had a "Fairfield Sentry" fund which was one of several dozen so-called feeder funds that gave foreign investors portals to Madoff. Fairfield, in turn, set up further feeder funds such as "'Lion Fairfield Capital

Management" in Singapore and "Stellar US Absolute Return", all ultimately conduits to Madoff, having directed a total of $7.5 billion, one-half of its total assets.[67] It is believed that only 2 of the at least 14 existing feeder funds overseas, have been exposed,[75] along with the known domestic ones.

Madoff was able to pitch his business acumen in Europe and South America, mostly indirectly through Fairfield fund founder, Walter Noel's son-in-law Andrés Piedrahita's connections.[76] Another Noel son-in-law's territory included Asia, most recently targeting China. Madoff was advertising to anyone with money (contrary to his initial strategy in which he handpicked investors).[67] The Madoff sales force were well-dressed, multilingual sales representatives in the financial capitals of Europe.[67]

Madoff's annual returns were "unusually consistent, "[76] around 10% and were a key factor in the perpetuation of the fraud for decades. Other Ponzi schemes may have paid returns of 20% or higher, typically collapsed quickly. One Madoff hedge fund, which described its "strategy" as focusing on shares in the Standard & Poor's 100-stock index, averaged a 10.5% annual return during the previous 17 years. Even at the end of November, 2008, amid a general market collapse, the same fund "reported" that it was up 5.6%, while the same year-to-date total return on the S&P 500-stock index had been negative (-) 38%.[17] An unnamed investor remarked, “The returns were just amazing and we trusted this guy for decades — if you wanted to take money out, you always got your check in a few days. That's why we were all so stunned."[63][77]

An invested Swiss bank, Union Bancaire Privée, explained that because of Madoff's huge volume as a broker-dealer, the bank believed he had a "perceived edge" on the market because his trades were timed well.[78]

4% Fee Structure

According to surreptitious investigator, Harry Markopolos, in order to deliver 12% annual returns to the investor, Madoff needed to earn 16% gross so he could pass on 4% to the feeder fund managers, who would lure in new victims, be "willfully blind, and not get too intrusive".[79]

Previous SEC Investigations

Madoff Securities LLC was investigated at least eight times in 16 years by the United States Securities and Exchange Commission (SEC) or other regulatory authorities.[80] In 1992, the SEC investigated one of Madoff's feeder funds, Avellino & Bienes (principals Frank Avellino and Michael Bienes and his wife Dianne Bienes), which invested solely with Madoff.[59]

Represented by Ira Lee Sorkin, Madoff's present attorney, Avellino & Bienes were accused of selling unregistered securities, and in its report the SEC mentioned the fund's "curiously steady" promised yearly returns to investors of 13.5% to 20%. However, the SEC did not look any more deeply into the matter.[59] Through Mr. Sorkin, the lawyer who once oversaw the regulator's New York office, the men agreed to return the money to investors, shut down their firm, undergo an audit and pay a fine of $350,000. Avellino then complained to the presiding Federal Judge, John E. Sprizzo, that Price Waterhouse fees were excessive. In April, 1993, the Judge ordered him to pay the bill of $428,679 in full. However, by the end of January, 1993, Mr. Sorkin and Mr. Avellino managed to curtail the audit, even though the judge concluded that Mr. Avellino had not been a credible witness in the case.[1] Both the securities investigation and the Price Waterhouse audit were effectively over.[59] At the time, Madoff said that he did not realize the feeder fund was operating illegally and that his own investment returns tracked the previous 10 years of the S&P 500.[59] Avellino & Bienes, previously an accounting firm, had turned to full-time investments in 1984 in a partnership with Madoff.[59] At the time of the investigation, the SEC did not publicly name Madoff because he was not accused of wrongdoing.[81] Michael Bienes later became a philanthropist donating at least $30 million in Florida and the United Kingdom, with a news report explaining that he "got lucky on the New York Stock Exchange."[82] Avellino has recently been sued by several Nantucket residents for investing their money with Madoff.[83] The 1992 incident was the first public indication that Madoff was placing orders for other funds.[80]

The SEC looked into Madoff in 1999 and 2000 about concerns that the firm was hiding its customers' orders from other traders, for which Madoff then took corrective measures.[80] In 2001, an SEC official met with financial investigator Harry Markopolos at the SEC's Boston office to go over Markopolos's allegations that Madoff's firm was engaged in fraudulent practices.[80] The SEC also said it conducted two inquiries of Madoff in the last several years and did not find major problems.[84] In 2004, after published articles appeared accusing the firm of front running, the SEC's Washington branch cleared Madoff of that accusation.[80] An SEC statement detailed that inspectors examined Madoff's brokerage operation in 2005 after sending the 2004 inquiry to the New York office,[80] finding three violations: the strategy he used for customer accounts, the requirement of brokers to obtain the best possible price for customer orders, and violating SEC rules by operating as an unregistered investment adviser. He was registered as a broker-dealer, but acting as an asset manager.[85] "The staff found no evidence of fraud," according to the SEC case memo. Mr. Madoff agreed to register his business that September, and the SEC did not make its findings public.[86] During the 2005 investigation, Meaghan Cheung, a branch head of the SEC's New York's Enforcement Division was the person responsible for the oversight and blunder, according to Harry Markopolos.[87] On February 4, 2009, he testified before the United States Congress at a hearing held by a House Financial Services Subcommittee on Capital Markets,[88][89][90] and will be interviewed on CBS's 60 Minutes.[91] In 2007, SEC enforcement staff completed an investigation into whether Madoff was running a Ponzi scheme and did not find any fraud or refer the matter to the SEC commissioners for legal action.[92][93]

The SEC has been accused of missing numerous red flags and ignoring tips on Madoff's alleged fraud.[94] As a result, the SEC's chairman Christopher Cox stated that an investigation will delve into "all staff contact and relationships with the Madoff family and firm, and their impact, if any, on decisions by staff regarding the firm."[95] A former SEC compliance officer, Eric Swanson, married Madoff's niece Shana, a Madoff firm compliance attorney.[95]

Red Flags

Outside analysts raised concerns with Madoff's firm for years.[17] Financial analyst Harry Markopolos complained to the SEC's Boston office in May 1999, telling the SEC staff they should investigate Madoff because it was impossible to legally make the profits Madoff claimed using the investment strategies that he claimed to use. In 2005, Markopolos sent a detailed 17 page memo directly to the SEC, entitled The World's Largest Hedge Fund is a Fraud.[96]

The paper specifies 29 numbered red flags. In part, the memo concluded: "Bernie Madoff is running the world's largest unregistered hedge fund. He's organized this business as 'hedge fund of funds privately labeling their own hedge funds which Bernie Madoff secretly runs for them using a split-strike conversion strategy getting paid only trading commissions which are not disclosed.' If this is not a regulatory dodge, I do not know what is." Markopolos concluded that Madoff's "unsophisticated portfolio management"[97] was either a Ponzi scheme or front running, placing favored orders before others when placing them in the market, but concluded it was most likely a Ponzi scheme.[80] An article in Barron's and another in MarHedge in 2001 accused Madoff of front running to achieve his gains.[80] Hedge funds who invested with him, were not allowed to mention his name in their marketing materials. Yet as Markopolos said, if you ran the world's most successful investment operation, would not you want that fact bruited far and wide in order to increase your business? The reason for Madoff's secrecy says Markopolos, was so that the SEC would not learn what he was doing. And to further maintain secrecy, when huge investors were thinking of putting in money, but wanted to examine Madoff's books in order to do due diligence, which they of course could afford, Madoff would not allow the examination, claiming a desire not to have proprietary strategies disclosed to any one else.[98]

Among the suspicious signs was the fact that Madoff's company avoided filing disclosures of its holdings with the SEC by selling its holdings for cash at the end of each period.[17] Such a tactic is highly unusual. It was Peter Madoff, Chief Compliance Officer, "for reasons of secrecy," who performed the audits.[99] Madoff's "official" three-person based [auditing firm, Friehling & Horowitz, had only one active accountant. Friehling & Horowitz has reported since 1993, in writing, to the American Institute of Certified Public Accountants that it does not conduct audits. At the time, New York State did not require peer review of accounting firms, but soon after it broke the magnitude of the scandal resulted in the state legislature requiring peer review.[100] David Friehling assumed control of the firm from partner Jerry Horowitz, his father-in-law, who reportedly did accounting work for Madoff for decades.[49][101] In 2007, hedge fund advisory fund firm], Aksia LLC advised its clients not to invest with Madoff, because of the appearance of limited accounting service personnel.[102][101] While hedge funds typically hold their portfolio at a securities firm that acts as the fund's prime broker (typically a major bank or brokerage), allowing an outside investigator to verify their holdings, Madoff's firm was its own broker-dealer and supposedly processed all its trades.[63]

Although Madoff was a pioneer of electronic trading, he refused to provide his clients online access to their accounts.[17] He sent out account statements by mail,[103] whereas most hedge funds email statements and allowed them to be downloaded via computer for easier analysis by investors.[40]

Improbably steady investment returns despite exceedingly volatile markets were another red flag.[104] A longtime friend said that "his rate of return [...] was never attention-grabbing, just solid 12–13% year in, year out".[18] Robert Ivanhoe, chairman of the real estate practice of the law firm Greenberg Traurig, added that Madoff increased his allure by refusing some investors.[18]

Charles Gradante, co-founder of hedge-fund research firm Hennessee Group, observed that Madoff "only had five down months since 1996",[105] and commented on Madoff's investment performance: "You cannot go 10 or 15 years with only three or four down months. It's just impossible."[104] A 2001 story in MARHedge interviewed traders who questioned how Madoff could have 72 gaining months in a row, saying that type of stock success had never occurred before.[15]

Madoff also operated as a broker dealer with an asset management division. Joe Aaron, a longtime hedge fund professional, found the structure suspicious and in 2003 warned a colleague to steer clear of the fund, saying "Why would a good businessman work his magic for pennies on the dollar?"[106]

At the same time as potential investors such as Société Générale were finding red flags from Madoff's firm, clients such as Fairfield and Union Bancaire Privée claimed that they had been given an "unusual degree of access" to look into Madoff's funds and had seen nothing wrong with his firm's investments.[76]

Recently, it has been suggested in research conducted by RiskData, that Madoff's series of returns were analytically similar to those of other funds which had previously been found to have engaged in deception and fraud. An investor making a simple calculation of the Bias ratio (finance) of Madoff's returns, should have been able to see that the performance series showed similarities to funds (e.g. Bayou) where the reported returns were ficticious and not linked to the uncertainties inherent in security price movement.

Whistleblower Harry Markopolos later testified to Congress that he had approached the Wall Street Journal about the existence of the Ponzi scheme in 2005. However, its editors decided not to pursue the story.[107]

Signs of Trouble

Early indications that Madoff may have been in trouble emerged in 2007. The Madoff Family Foundation donated only $95,000 to charitable groups. This was a major drop from previous years. In 2006, the foundation had donated $1,277,600.[108]

The scheme began to unravel in late 2008, as the stock market began to plunge. Subsequently, as the general market downturn accelerated, a barrage of investors requested to withdraw money. They attempted to withdraw $7 billion from the firm, and in the days and weeks prior to his arrest, Madoff struggled to keep the scheme afloat. To pay off those investors, Mr. Madoff needed new money from other investors.

Madoff received $250 million around December 1 from Carl J. Shapiro, a 95-year-old Boston philanthropist and entrepreneur who is one of Madoff's oldest friends and biggest financial backers. On December 5, he accepted $10 million from Martin Rosenman, president of Rosenman Family LLC, who wants to recover a never-invested $10 million, deposited in a Madoff account at JPMorgan, wired six days before Madoff's arrest. Bankruptcy Judge Lifland ruled that the Rosenman lawsuit will be dealt with separately.[109]

Madoff also asked others for money in the final weeks before his arrest, including Wall Street financier Kenneth Langone, whose office was sent a 19-page pitch-book, allegedly created by the staff at the Fairfield Greenwich Group. Madoff said he was raising money for a new investment vehicle, between $500 million and $1 billion for exclusive clients. He said he was moving quickly on the venture and wanted an answer by the following week. Langone declined.[110]

On December 10, 2008, he suggested to his sons, Mark and Andrew, that the firm pay out several million dollars in bonuses two months ahead of schedule, from $200 million in assets that the firm still had.[15] According to the complaint, Mark and Andrew, reportedly unaware of the firm's pending insolvency, confronted their father, asking him how the firm could pay bonuses to employees if it could not pay investors. Madoff then admitted that he was "finished" and that the asset management arm of the firm was in fact a Ponzi scheme. Mark and Andrew then reported him to the authorities.[17]

To date, the FBI investigation has discovered no evidence implicating family members of fraud,[111] and federal authorities report his wife Ruth is not accused of wrongdoing.[112]

Charges

Criminal

Madoff was arrested by the Federal Bureau of Investigation (FBI) on December 11, 2008 on criminal charges of securities fraud. The previous day, he had told his sons that his business was "a giant Ponzi scheme."[113][114] They called a friend for advice, Martin Flumenbaum, a lawyer, who called federal prosecutors and the SEC on their behalf. FBI's Agent Theodore Cacioppi made a house call. "We are here to find out if there is an innocent explanation," Cacioppi said quietly. The 70-year-old financier paused, "There is no innocent explanation."[115][116] He had "paid investors with money that was not there."[60] The New York Times has reported that Madoff's lawyer, Ira Sorkin, has confirmed in a court filing that Madoff confessed.[8]

The criminal complaint alleges that investors lost $50 billion through the scheme,[116] though The Wall Street Journal reports "that figure includes the alleged false profits that Mr. Madoff's firm reported to its customers for decades. It's unclear exactly how much investors deposited into the firm."[117] He was charged with a single count of securities fraud. He faces up to 20 years in prison and a fine of $5 million if convicted.[113] His attorney, Ira Sorkin, who was also an investor,[118] stated that Madoff "will fight to get through this unfortunate set of events."

The criminal case is U.S. v. Madoff, 08-MAG-02735, U.S. District Court for the Southern District of New York (Manhattan) with presiding Judge Ronald L. Ellis.[43] Apart from 'Bernard L. Madoff' and 'Bernard L. Madoff Investment Securities LLC ("BMIS")', the order to freeze all activities[119] also forbids acting and trading from the companies Madoff Securities International Ltd. ("Madoff International") and Madoff Ltd.

Madoff was released on the same day of his arrest after posting $10 million bail.[113] Madoff and his wife have surrendered their passports, and he at first was subject to travel restrictions, a 7 p.m. curfew at his co-op, and electronic monitoring as a condition of bail. Although Madoff only had two co-signers for his $10 million bail, his wife and his brother Peter, rather than the four required, a judge allowed him free on bail but ordered him confined to his penthouse.[120] Madoff wears an electronic ankle bracelet to ensure compliance.[120] Madoff has reportedly received death threats that have been referred to the FBI, and the SEC referred to fears of "harm or flight" in its request for Madoff to be confined to his Upper East Side apartment.[120][121] Cameras will monitor the apartment's doors, its communication devices will send signals to the FBI, and his wife will be required to pay for additional security.[121]

Prosecutors asked on January 5, 2009, that his bail be revoked, after Madoff and his wife allegedly violated a court-ordered asset freeze by mailing jewelry worth up to $1 million to relatives, including their sons and Madoff's brother. It was also noted that $173 million in signed checks had been found in Madoff's office desk after he had been arrested.[122][123] His sons reported the mailings to prosecutors. Previously, Madoff was thought to be cooperating with prosecutors.[123] The following week, the Judge Ellis refused the government's request to jail Madoff, but required as a condition of bail that Madoff make an inventory of personal items and that his mail be searched.[124]

Civil

On February 9, 2009, a partial judgment in the December 11, 2008 civil suit, SEC v. Madoff, 08-10791, U.S. District Court, Southern District of New York (Manhattan) was made permanent.[125] Madoff will keep a previously reached agreement to freeze his assets, and neither work in the financial industry ever again, nor violate any other securities laws. The agreement does not require Madoff to admit or deny any allegations against him. It also leaves the issues of any civil fines and repayments to be imposed against Madoff for a later time. [126] Without reaching an agreement, he would have had to testify or refuse. This settlement is unrelated to any plea or indictment in the criminal matter.[127]

Others Involved

Investigators are looking for others involved in the scheme, despite Madoff's statement that he alone was responsible for the large-scale operation.[14] Harry Sussman, an attorney representing several clients of the firm, stated that "someone had to create the appearance that there were returns," and further suggested that there must have been a team buying and selling stocks, forging books, and filing reports.[14]

Federal investigators have discovered apparently fraudulent documents and records in Madoff's Manhattan offices, and are looking into who prepared them.[14] The role of Frank DiPascali, an official at the firm, is being considered. DiPascali is represented by Marc Mukasey, the son of former U.S. Attorney General Michael Mukasey, who has recused himself of any involvement in the case. Mr. DiPascali joined Mr. Madoff's operation in 1975, having been introduced by a neighbor in Howard Beach, Queens, N.Y. He researched stocks for the Madoff firm's trading desk before joining Madoff's separate investment-advisory business. He referred to himself as "director of options trading" and also as "chief financial officer". According to an SEC memo, DiPascali "responded evasively" to questioning following Madoff's arrest.[117] In addition to his own contact with clients, Mr. DiPascali supervised a group of about six other employees involved in taking and keeping track of client orders. Investors spoke to these other employees and would fax orders if they needed to withdraw money. DiPascali's name was sometimes given as an alternate contact. Mr. DiPascali provided investors with instructions for wiring money.[128]

Madoff's accountant was David G. Friehling, the only active accountant at Friehling & Horowitz according to the AICPA. The accounting firm has informed the AICPA in writing for 15 years that it does not conduct audits.[129] An investigation into Friehling by Rockland County, New York district attorney Thomas Zugibe was stopped in deferral to the investigation by the US Attorney's office out of Manhattan.[101]

J. Ezra Merkin, a prominent investment advisor and philanthropist, has been sued for his role in running a "feeder fund" for Madoff.[130] Merkin informed investors in his $1.8 billion Ascot Partners fund on December 11 that he was among those who suffered substantial personal losses, since all of the fund's money was invested with Madoff.[131] The Connecticut Attorney General Richard Blumenthal is examining the role boards of nonprofits played, in possibly not conducting due diligence with donors' contributions.[132]On January 15, 2009, as part of a probe into Madoff and New York nonprofits which claim they were defrauded, New York State Attorney General Andrew Cuomo issued subpoenas to three investment funds run by Merkin, and 15 nonprofits which say they lost money due to Merkin and Madoff.[133]

Regulators are looking into a brokerage firm, Cohmad Securities (taken from the names "Cohn" and "Madoff"), which is largely owned by Maurice Cohn ("Sonny") and his daughter Marcia, President and Chief Compliance Officer, of whom Madoff shares 10-20% ownership stakes, and Madoff's firm's address in New York City. Peter Madoff, brother of Bernard, owns less than one share. Cohmad employs Robert Jaffe, as vice president, whose ownership was less than 5%.[134] Jaffe is married to Ellen Shapiro, daughter of Boston philanthropist Carl J. Shapiro, the founder and former chairman of apparel company Kay Windsor Inc. and an early investor and close friend of Madoff. Jaffe reportedly convinced the elder Shapiro to invest $250 million with Madoff just ten days before Madoff's arrest.[135]

Jaffe, a bon vivant and philanthropist, worked the Palm Beach, Florida circuit, and attracted many Palm Beach Country Club members as investors."[39] Jaffe said he received a commission of 1% to 2% from an investor's first profit after he guided their money to Madoff. Jaffe paid commissions to financial advisers who steered cash to Madoff's fund.[136][137]

On January 14, 2009, William Galvin, Secretary of the Commonwealth of Massachusetts who is in charge of securities issues for Massachusetts, filed suit against Jaffe, the Cohmad broker for Madoff, who promoted Madoff's funds to wealthy investors in Massachusetts and Florida.[138][139] Richard Spring, of Boca Raton, Florida, received payments from Cohmad for many years, in exchange for bringing investors and investment ideas to Madoff. Alvin J. "Sonny" Delaire Jr., whose late father, Alvin J. Delaire was a partner with Sonny Cohn in a previous venture, also recruited clients for Madoff's advisory business. Cohmad had fewer than 650 client accounts, made 99.7% of its sales from brokerage services to Madoff's larger broker-dealer. In its audited financial statements for the 12 months ending June 30, 2008, Cohmad said revenue from Madoff Securities totalled

$3,736,829. Its total sales for the same period were $3,748,397.[134][140]

Stanley Chais, 82, a wealthy investment advisor from Beverly Hills, California was accused of steering money to private interests, including Madoff, through Chais's Brighton Co., a limited partnership formed to manage money. He took about 3.8% of the profits as management fees. His Chais Family Foundation, which in 2007 reported assets of $178 million and charitable contributions of nearly $8.2 million, was wiped out and has shut down. He had an unpretentious home in Beverly Hills, a small apartment in New York and drove an old Toyota. Michael Chaleff, a former Justice Department lawyer, was part of a 50-member investment group called CMG that lost $75 million to $80 million it gave to Chais' Brighton Co. Chaleff has filed a $250-million class action federal lawsuit against Chais in Los Angeles, as has Academy Award-winning screenwriter Eric Roth, recently nominated for a Golden Globe award for The Curious Case of Benjamin Button.[141][142] New Jersey state Senator Loretta Weinberg lost her entire life savings in Chais' "Arbitrage Partnerships" fund.[143][144]

Recovery of Funds

Madoff's assets have been frozen, and he has been ordered to develop a list of his clients.[121] The victims of the alleged fraud are considering how to best recover some of their investments.[145] The SEC filed a separate civil suit against Madoff on December 11, 2008.[43][146] Separately, individual investors have filed civil suits against Madoff. The two firms leading the suits announced on December 12, 2008 that the firms have been retained by dozens of individual investors.[147] Investors may also have access to funds from the Securities Investor Protection Corporation (SIPC), a securities-industry group formed by Congress to help customers of failed brokerages firms. SIPC has $1.7 billion in assets, $1 billion in credit available from the U.S. Treasury and another credit line from several international banks.[148] Investors may receive a maximum of $500,000 from SIPC, but only for cash or securities that are missing from their accounts. It could take several years before investigations into the scandal are concluded and investors are able to file claims.[149][150] Victims may also file suit to have taxes already paid on "fictitious income" restored to them.[151][152][150] Victims may also file suit to have taxes already paid on "fictitious income" restored to them.[151][153]

On January 6, 2009, the court-appointed trustee of the Madoff firm, Irving Picard, and lawyers from his firm, Baker Hostetler LLP (a Cleveland-based firm Picard joined the week before he was appointed), who are locating assets for distribution to investors, said some investors may get cash advances from SIPC, well before March 4, 2009.[110] U.S. District Judge Lawrence McKenna gave Picard power to seize assets and records, demand documents, summon witnesses and enter Madoff's residences around the world, including the apartment where he's under house arrest. As of February 4, 2009, Picard has reported that approximately $946.4 million in cash and securities has been recovered,[154] which includes The Bank of New York Mellon Corp's is $301,407,190 in one Madoff company account and JP Morgan Chase's $233,500,000 in three accounts.[155] Picard will terminate Madoff's leases totaling $ 117,359 of a 2007 Land Rover, 2008 Cadillac, 2007, 2008, and 2009 Mercedes-Benzes and a 2006 Lexus.[156] On January 2, he sent letters to 8,000 potential claimants, customers who have until March 2, and creditors, until July 2 to place claims.[157]

On October 31, 2008, Craig Kugel, human resource employee, was "designated" a trustee by Peter B. Madoff, who told him to sign a lease for his brother, as guarantor for a Mercedes S-550, because Madoff refused to provide the requisite company credit information. A Bankruptcy Court Judge Burton Lifland denied Kugel's estimated remaining $ 58,212 lease liability.[158][159]

The SIPC case is Securities Investor Protection Corp. v. Bernard L. Madoff Investment Securities LLC, 08-01789, U.S. Bankruptcy Court, Southern District of New York (Manhattan). The criminal case is U.S.A. v. Madoff, 1:08-mj-02735, and the SEC case is Securities and Exchange Commission v. Madoff, 1:08-cv- 10791, both U.S. District Court, Southern District of New York (Manhattan).[160]

The cases against Fairfield Greenwich Group et al are consolidated as 09-118 in U.S. District Court for the Southern District of New York (Manhattan)[161]

The use of the legal doctrine of fraudulent conveyance in bankruptcy proceedings might mean that investors who withdrew their money before the fraud was revealed might be forced to return their profits or even part of their initial investments. Returning funds would be uncontroversial for clients who knew that Madoff's business was fraudulent, but would not be so clear for clients who were unaware of Madoff's activities.[162][163] For example, Hadassah may be forced by New York State law to return some portion of the $130 million it withdrew from the funds it invested with Madoff.[164][163] For example, Hadassah may be forced by New York State law to return some portion of the $130 million it withdrew from the funds it invested with Madoff.[165] The current statute of limitations on cases involving fraudulent conveyance is up to six years.

Madoff provided a list of his and his firm's assets to the SEC on December 31. The list was kept confidential by the SEC, on the grounds that the court did not authorize disclosure. Prof. John Coffee, of Columbia University Law School, said that much of Madoff's money may be in offshore funds, and that the SEC wanted to keep the assets secret to keep them from being seized by foreign regulators and foreign creditors.[166][167]

Affected Clients

On February 4, 2009, the 162-page client list with "thousands" of names[168] (without investment amount) filing was released by the U.S. Bankruptcy Court in Manhattan, of which, some have profited. The many individual investors who invested through Fairfield Greenwich, Ascot Partners, and Chais Investments are not included on the list.[169][170][171]

The clients included banks, hedge funds, charities, universities and wealthy individuals who have disclosed about $41 billion invested with Bernard L. Madoff Investment Securities LLC, according to a Bloomberg News tally.[148]

Although Madoff filed a report with the SEC in 2008 stating that his advisory business had only 11–25 clients and about $17.1 billion in assets,[172] dozens of investors have reported losses, and Madoff estimated the fraud at $50 billion. According to Bloomberg, "in all, companies, individuals and foundations have disclosed about $24 billion of investments with Madoff."[173] Those affected include banks, Wall Street investors, charities, as well as individuals. On February 4, 2009, federal courts in New York released a 162-page list of Madoff clients, with thousands of names on the list.[174]

The large sovereign wealth fund Abu Dhabi Investment Authority indirectly invested $400 million with Madoff.

Other notable clients included former Salomon Brothers economist Henry Kaufman, Steven Spielberg, Jeffrey Katzenberg, actors Kevin Bacon and wife Kyra Sedgwick, actor John Malkovich, and Zsa Zsa Gabor.[175] Mortimer Zuckerman lost approximately $30 million of his charitable trust fund.[176] At a forum at the YIVO Institute for Jewish Research in New York, Zuckerman remarked, no one since Julius Rosenberg, executed in 1953 along with his wife, Ethel, for giving atomic secrets to the Soviet Union, "has so damaged the image and self respect of American Jews."[177]

Several charities invested all or part of their endowments with Madoff, and the revelation of the fraud forced them to shut down. Additionally, the Lappin Foundation had invested its employee 401(k) with Madoff; it is presumed that the employees' retirement accounts have been completely voided.

Largest Stake-Holders

According to The Wall Street Journal[178] the investors with the largest potential losses include:

Fairfield Greenwich Advisors, $7.50 billion

Tremont Capital Management, $3.30 billion

Banco Santander, $2.87 billion

Bank Medici, $2.10 billion

Ascot Partners, $1.80 billion

Access International Advisors, $1.40 billion

Fortis, $1.35 billion

HSBC, $1.00 billion

The potential losses of these eight investors total $21.32 billion.

Other investors, with potential losses between $100 million and $1 billion include:

Natixis SA

Carl J. Shapiro (a 95-year-old Boston philanthropist)

Royal Bank of Scotland Group PLC

BNP Paribas

BBVA

Man Group PLC

Reichmuth & Co.

Nomura Holdings

Aozora Bank[179]

Maxam Capital Management

EIM SA

AXA SA

Union Bancaire Privée

Jerome Fisher, co-founder of Nine West Shoes has lost $150 million with Madoff, according to the Palm Beach Post.[180]

Twenty-three investors with potential losses of $500,000 to $100 million were also listed, with total potential losses of $540 million. They included Bramdean Alternatives run by Nicola Horlick, for example. The grand total potential losses in the Wall Street Journal table is $26.9 billion.

On December 24, 2008, Bloomberg News listed financial losses related to Madoff's fraud totaling $36 billion, which may include double counting from investors in feeder funds.[181][182] A partial list of Madoff's victims from the Bloomberg report includes US Senator Frank Lautenberg's charitable foundation, the Horowitz

Association at $800 million, $696 million in losses to Notz, Stucki & Cie, up to $614 million to Natixis SA, BNP Paribas SA at up to $478.2 million, $400 million in losses to Fix Asset Management, and $302 million in losses to Nomura Holdings Inc..[181]

On January 15, 2009, the website Swissinfo.ch reported that French wealth management group Oddo et Cie sued Swiss bank UBS AG on January 14, 2009 in court in Luxembourg for €30 million (US$39.5 million) over losses allegedly due to UBS exposure to Madoff's firm.[183]

On January 20, 2009, French prosecutors opened an investigation on behalf of French citizens and institutions who claim losses due to Madoff. One part of the investigation is over the AlphaLux fund set up by UBS, which counters that the bank set up the Luxembourg-based fund at the request of investors, but that Madoff was never on UBS's list of preferred investments. French prosecutors speculate that the total exposure to Madoff by French investors might be as high as €500 million.[184]

On January 21, 2009, Jacques Rauber, head of Auriga International Advisers, a hedge fund based in the British Virgin Islands, said in an interview in the Swiss newspaper Sonntag Zeitung that his fund lost over $350 million due to exposure to Madoff's firm.[185]

Some investors have amended their initial estimates of losses to include only their original investment, since the profits Madoff reported to them which they were including were most likely fraudulent. Yeshiva University, for instance, said its actual incurred loss was its invested $14.5 million, not the $110 million initially estimated, which included alleged profits reported to the university by Madoff.[186]

Impact and Aftermath

Suicide of Client

On December 23, 2008, one of the founders of Access International Advisors LLC, René-Thierry Magon de la Villehuchet, was found dead in his company office on Madison Avenue in New York City. His left wrist was slit[187] and de la Villehuchet had taken sleeping pills, in what appeared to be suicide.[188][189]

Harry Markopolos said he met Mr. de La Villehuchet many years ago through a more junior colleague at Access, and he subsequently warned him that Madoff might be committing illegal acts.[190] According to Markopolos, Access was majority owned by noblemen whose ancestors served as Napoleon's military officers. Access partner Philippe Junot is the former husband of Princess Caroline of Monaco, and Prince Michael of Yugoslavia was an investor relations executive. In 2002, Access invested about 45% of its $1.2 billion under management with Madoff. By 2008, it managed $3 billion and raised the proportion of funds with Madoff to about 75%. De la Villehuchet had also invested all of his wealth and 20% of his brother, Bertrand's with Madoff.[191] He lived in New Rochelle, New York and came from a very prominent French family. Although no suicide note was found at the scene, his brother in France received a note shortly after his death in which he expressed remorse and a feeling of responsibility.[187] The FBI and SEC do not believe de la Villehuchet was involved in the fraud.[189]

Philanthropy

Before his arrest, Madoff's family was involved in philanthropic circles.[18] When his nephew, Roger Madoff, died of leukemia in April 2006, paid death notices appeared in newspapers from a range of charitable organizations, including the Lower East Side Tenement Museum.[18] Madoff donated approximately $6 million to lymphoma research after his son Andrew was diagnosed.[108]

Madoff served as the Chairman of the Board of Directors] of the Sy Syms School of Business at Yeshiva University, as well as Treasurer of its Board of Trustees.[18][19] He resigned his position at Yeshiva University after his arrest.[19] Madoff also serves on the Board of New York City Center, a member of New York City's Cultural Institutions Group (CIG).[192] He served on the executive council of the Wall Street division of the UJA Foundation of New York, a Jewish foundation which declined to invest funds with him due to the conflict of interest.[193]

Madoff undertook charity work for the Gift of Life Bone Marrow Foundation, a charity he allegedly defrauded at the same time for $2 million according to The New York Times, and also engaged in philanthropic giving through The Madoff Family Foundation, a $19 million private foundation, which he managed along with his wife.[17] They donated money to hospitals and theaters.[18] The foundation has also contributed to many educational, cultural, and health charities, including those later forced to close due to Madoff's alleged malfeasance. The various organizations were mostly given charity funds backed by Madoff securities.[19][22] Madoff was also a contributor to the Democratic Party, donating about $25,000 a year.[15][194]

Madoff and his immediate family have given overwhelmingly to Democrat candidates according to records at [2] In the wake of Madoff's arrest, the assets of the Madoff Family Foundation have been frozen by a federal court.[17][19]

References

* "Wall Street legend Bernard Madoff arrested over '$50 billion Ponzi scheme'". Times Online. Times Newspapers Ltd.. December 12, 2008. http://www.timesonline.co.uk/tol/news/world/us_and_americas/article5331997.ece. Retrieved on December 13, 2008.

* Amir Efrati (2009-01-12). "Madoff Prosecutors Push Back Deadline". The Wall Street Journal. http://online.wsj.com/article/SB123172283787772497.html?mod=googlenews_wsj. Retrieved on 2009-01-29.

* David Voreacos and David Glovin (2008-12-13). "Madoff Confessed $50 Billion Fraud Before FBI Arrest". Bloomberg News. http://www.bloomberg.com/apps/news?pid=newsarchive&sid=atUk.QnXAvZY.

* Binyamin Appelbaum, David S. Hilzenrath and Amit R. Paley (2008-12-13). "It was all one big lie. Bernard Madoff was a Wall Street whiz with a golden reputation. Investors, including Jewish charities, entrusted him with billions. It's gone.". Washington Post. p. D01. http://www.washingtonpost.com/wp-dyn/content/article/2008/12/12/AR2008121203970_pf.html. Retrieved on 18 January 2009.

* "SEC: Complaint SEC against Madoff and BMIS LLC" (PDF). U.S. Securities and Exchange Commission. December 11, 2008. http://www.sec.gov/litigation/complaints/2008/comp-madoff121108.pdf. Retrieved on December 29, 2008.

* "Former Nasdaq chairman charged with fraud". CNN. 11 December 2008. http://edition.cnn.com/2008/US/12/11/madoff.arrest/?iref=mpstoryview. Retrieved on 16 December 2008.

* "S.E.C. Updates on Madoff Case; Charities Feel Losses". Politonomist.com. 18 December 2008. http://www.politonomist.com/s-updates-on-madoff-case-charities-feel-losses-00133/. Retrieved on 3 January 2009.

* Diana Henriques (2009-01-13). "New Description of Timing on Madoff's Confession". New York Times. http://www.nytimes.com/2009/01/10/business/10madoff.html. Retrieved on 19 January 2009.

* Larson. "U.S. Judge Freezes Madoff Assets, Appoints Receiver, SEC Says". Bloomberg.com (Bloomberg News). http://www.bloomberg.com/apps/news?pid=20601087&sid=a.9m_dUE2Pxc&refer=home.

* "SEC Charges Bernard L. Madoff for Multi-Billion Dollar Ponzi Scheme (2008-293)". SEC.gov. U.S. Securities and Exchange Commission. December 11,

2008. http://www.sec.gov/news/press/2008/2008-293.htm. Retrieved on December 11, 2008.

* "Rich investors 'wiped out' by Wall Street fraud". The Independent. 14 December 2008. http://www.independent.co.uk/news/world/americas/rich-investors-wiped-out-by-wall-street-fraud-1066090.html. Retrieved on 17 December 2008.

* "US fraud scheme to cost Spanish savers more than three billion: press". Agence France Press. December 13, 2008. http://www.google.com/hostednews/afp/article/ALeqM5h8dkhwUDmjZhbvCsbADor874kklA. Retrieved on December 23, 2008.

* "HSBC says Madoff potential exposure $1 billion". Reuters. December 15, 2008. http://uk.reuters.com/article/businessNews/idUKTRE4BE3E120081215. Retrieved on December 23, 2008.

* Caruso, David (18 December 2008). "Madoff Investigators Look for Partners". Associated Press (AOL). http://news.aol.com/article/did-bernard-madoff-act-alone-investors/281857. Retrieved on 23 December 2008.

* Lieberman, David; Pallavi Gogoi, Theresa Howard, Kevin McCoy, Matt Krantz (15 December 2008). "Investors remain amazed over Madoff's sudden downfall". USA Today.

http://www.usatoday.com/money/markets/2008-12-14-ponzi-madoff-downfall_N.htm. Retrieved on 24 December 2008.

* O'Hara, Maureen (1995). Market Microstructure Theory. Oxford: Blackwell. p. 190. ISBN 1-55786-443-8. http://books.google.com/books?id=gHrzgo0ghfMC&pg=PA190&lpg=PA190&dq=madoff+securities+maureen+o%27hara&source=web&ots=pYJvd_jmOd&sig=l9ZhWlP_w_ImYe8j6onWPTclqCI&hl=en&sa=X&oi=book_result&resnum=7&ct=result. Retrieved on December 16, 2008.

* Appelbaum, Binyamin; David S. Hilzenrath and Amit R. Paley (13 December 2008). "'All Just One Big Lie'". The Washington Post (Washington Post Company): p. D01. http://www.washingtonpost.com/wp-dyn/content/article/2008/12/12/AR2008121203970.html?hpid=topnews. Retrieved on 12 December 2008.

* "Standing Accused: A Pillar of Finance and Charity". The New York Times. 13 December 2008. http://www.nytimes.com/2008/12/13/nyregion/13madoff.html?_r=1&ref=nyregion.

* "Madoff Wall Street fraud threatens Jewish philanthropy". http://www.haaretz.com/hasen/spages/1046187.html. Retrieved on 13 December 2008.

* Henriques. "For Investors, Trust Lost, and Money Too". The New York Times. http://www.nytimes.com/2008/12/13/business/13investors.html?pagewanted=all. Retrieved on 13 December 2008.

* "Two More Charities Announce Closing Due to Madoff" AP via Yahoo! News.

* Sherwell. "Bernie Madoff: Profile of a Wall Street star". Telegraph. http://www.telegraph.co.uk/finance/3742427/Bernie-Madoff-Profile-of-a-Wall-Street-star.html. Retrieved on 14 December 2008.

* Madoffwatch. "It Was a Family Thing, Apparently". cityfile. http://cityfile.com/dailyfile/3953. Retrieved on 30 January 2009.

* Fortune. "Madoff's mother tangled with the feds". CNNMoney.com. http://money.cnn.com/2009/01/16/magazines/fortune/madoff_mother.fortune/index.htm. Retrieved on 30 January 2009.

* John Carney. "The Education of Bernie Madoff: The High School Years". Clusterstock. http://clusterstock.alleyinsider.com/2008/12/the-education-of-bernie-madoff-far-rockaway-high-school. Retrieved on 2008-12-25.

* Salkin, Allen (16 January 2009). "Bernie Madoff, Frat Brother". New York Times. http://www.nytimes.com/2009/01/18/fashion/18madoff.html. Retrieved on 20 January 2009.

* Chernoff (26 December 2008). "What drove Bernie Madoff". CNN. http://money.cnn.com/2008/12/26/news/companies/understanding_Madoff/?postversion=2008122608. Retrieved on 26 December 2008.

* Lambiet (12 December 2008). "Bernie Madoff's arrest sent tremors into Palm Beach". Palm Beach Daily. http://www.palmbeachdailynews.com/news/content/news/2008/12/12/ponzi1212.html. Retrieved on 12 December 2008.

* "A Madoff Cookbook Has a Secret, Too". http://www.nytimes.com/2009/01/15/business/15cook.html.

* "No |title= specified". http://online.wsj.com/article/SB123267210646108493.html?mod=googlenews_wsj.

* "Inquiry Finds No Signs Family Aided Madoff". The New York Times. 16 December 2008. http://www.nytimes.com/2008/12/16/business/16madoff.html?scp=20&sq=&st=nyt. Retrieved on 20 December 2008.

* |title=One Madoff charity goes unscathed | first =Eugenia | last =Levenson |date=December 17, 2008|work=CNNMoney.com |url=http://money.cnn.com/2008/12/17/news/companies/madoff_lymphoma.fortune/index.htm?postversion=2008121715

* "Inquiry Finds No Signs Family Aided Madoff". The New York Times. December 16, 2008. http://www.nypost.com/seven/02022009/gossip/pagesix/im_not_madoff_153188.htm. Retrieved on December 20, 2008.

* |title=One Madoff charity goes unscathed | first =Eugenia | last =Levenson |date=December 17, 2008|work=CNNMoney.com |url=http://money.cnn.com/2008/12/17/news/companies/madoff_lymphoma.fortune/index.htm?postversion=2008121715

* "No |title= specified". http://www.nypost.com/seven/02022009/gossip/pagesix/im_not_madoff_153188.htm.

* "www.independent.co.uk/news/business/analysis-and-features/the-madoff-files-the-man-behind-the-most-audacious-fraud-in-history-1518939.html". http://www.independent.co.uk/news/business/analysis-

and-features/the-madoff-files-the-man-behind-the-most-audacious-fraud-in-history-1518939.html.

* Maier, Kate (December 12, 2008). "Montauk Oceanfront Owner Cited in Ponzi Scheme". East Hampton Star. http://www.easthamptonstar.com/dnn/Home/News/MadoffinMontauk/tabid/7369/Default.aspx. Retrieved on December 23, 2008.

* Jagger, Suzy (December 18, 2008). "Bernard Madoff: the 'most hated man in New York' seeks $3 m for bail". The Times. http://business.timesonline.co.uk/tol/business/industry_sectors/banking_and_finance/article5362075.ece. Retrieved on December 23, 2008.

* Frank, Robert (December 13, 2008). "Fund Fraud Hits Big Names; Madoff's Clients Included Mets Owner, GMAC Chairman, Country-Club Recruits". Wall Street Journal. http://online.wsj.com/article/SB122914169719104017.html?mod=djemalertNEWS. Retrieved on December 13, 2008.

* "Wall Street Titan May Have Fooled Investors for Years". CNBC. http://www.cnbc.com/id/28198739. Retrieved on 13 December 2008.

* "Madoff's arrest in billion-dollar fraud case shocks Palm Beach investors" Palm Beach Post December 12, 2008.

* Creswell, Julie (24 January 2009). "The Talented Mr. Madoff". The New York Times. http://www.nytimes.com/2009/01/25/business/25bernie.html?em. Retrieved on 25 January 2009.

* Glovin, Dan; Bradley Keoun (11 December 2008). "Madoff Charged in $50 Billion Fraud at Investment Advisory Firm". Bloomberg News. http://www.bloomberg.com/apps/news?pid=20601087&sid=a8EVy7KVpBaA&refer=home. Retrieved on 11 December 2008.

* "www.independent.co.uk/news/business/analysis-and-features/the-madoff-files-the-man-behind-the-most-audacious-fraud-in-history-1518939.html". http://www.independent.co.uk/news/business/analysis-and-features/the-madoff-files-the-man-behind-the-most-audacious-fraud-in-history-1518939.html.

*
"www.jpost.com/servlet/Satellite?cid=1233304648603&pagename=JPost%2FJPArticle%2FShowFull". http://www.jpost.com/servlet/Satellite?cid=1233304648603&pagename=JPost%2FJPArticle%2FShowFull.

* de la Merced, Michael J. (24 December 2008). "Effort Under Way to Sell Madoff Unit". The New York Times.

http://www.nytimes.com/2008/12/25/business/25madoff.html. Retrieved on 24 December 2008.

* Weiner, Eric J. (2005). What Goes Up: The Uncensored History of Modern Wall Street as Told by the Bankers, Brokers, CEOs, and Scoundrels who Made it Happen. Little, Brown and Company. pp. 188–192. ISBN 0316929662. http://books.google.com/books?id=dIT4cjRNpygC&q=Madoff#search_anchor.

* "The Owner's Name is on the Door". Madoff.com. http://www.madoff.com/dis/display.asp?id=203&mode=1&home=1#owner. Retrieved on 2008-12-11. Archive

* Probe Eyes Role of Aide to Madoff, Accountant. Wall Street Journal, December 23, 2008.

* Kolker, Carlyn; Tiffany Kary and Saijel Kishan (23 December 2008). "Madoff Victims May Have to Return Profits, Principal". Bloomberg News. http://www.bloomberg.com/apps/news?pid=20601087&sid=awmAWSxKpXRM&refer=home. Retrieved on 24 December 2008.

* Wilhelm, William J.; Joseph D. Downing (2001). Information Markets: What Businesses Can Learn from Financial Innovation. Harvard Business Press. p. 153. ISBN 1578512786.

http://books.google.com/books?id=xVqgCFKxHvgC&q=Madoff#search_anchor.

* Princeton University Undergraduate Task Force (January 2005). "THE REGULATION OF PUBLICLY TRADED SECURITIES" (PDF). U.S. Securities and Exchange Commission. 58. http://www.sec.gov/rules/proposed/s71004/s71004-587.pdf. Retrieved on December 17, 2008.

* Harris, Larry (2003). Trading and Exchanges: Market Microstructure for Practitioners. Oxford University Press. p. 290. ISBN 0195144708. http://books.google.com/books?id=Rd9hDRR1Yx4C&q=Madoff#search_anchor.

* Ferrell, Allen (2001). "A Proposal for Solving the "Payment for Order Flow" Problem" (PDF). 74 S.Cal.L.Rev. 1027. Harvard. http://www.law.harvard.edu/faculty/fferrell/pdfs/payment_for_orderflow.pdf. Retrieved on December 12, 2008.

* Battalio, Robert H.; Tim Loughran (January 15, 2007). "Does Payment for Order Flow to Your Broker Help or Hurt You?" (PDF). Notre Dame University. http://www.nd.edu/~tloughra/Orderflow.pdf. Retrieved on December 12, 2008.

* McMillan, Alex (May 29, 2000). ""Q&A: Madoff Talks Trading". CNN.

http://money.CNN.com/2000/05/29/investing/q_madoff/. Retrieved on December 11, 2008.

* Henriques, Diana B.; Alex Berenson (14 December 2008). "The 17th Floor, Where Wealth Went to Vanish". The New York Times. http://www.nytimes.com/2008/12/15/business/15madoff.html. Retrieved on 23 December 2008.

* Dovkants, Keith; Alex Berenson (16 December 2008). "Revealed: Magic Madoff's family 'piggy bank' in the heart of Mayfair". Evening Standard. http://www.thisislondon.co.uk/standard/article-23602414-details/Revealed:+Magic+Madoff%E2%80%99s+family+%E2%80%98piggy+bank%E2%80%99+in+the+heart+of+Mayfair/article.do. Retrieved on 25 December 2008.

* Moyer, Liz (23 December 2008). "Could SEC Have Stopped Madoff Scam In 1992?". Forbes. http://www.forbes.com/business/2008/12/23/madoff-fraud-sec-biz-wall-cx_lm_1223madoff.html. Retrieved on 24 December 2008.

* Honan, Edith (December 12, 2008). "Former Nasdaq chair arrested over alleged £33 billion fraud". International Herald Tribune. http://www.iht.com/articles/reuters/2008/12/12/business/OUKBS-UK-MADOFF-ARREST.php. Retrieved on December 12, 2008.

* Arvedlund, Erin E. (7 May 2001). "Do not Ask, Do not Tell". Barron's Magazine (Dow Jones). http://online.barrons.com/article/SB989019667829349012.html. Retrieved on 23 December 2008.

* Interview with Jim Voss Bloomberg

* "Look at Wall St. Wizard Finds Magic Had Skeptics". The New York Times. 13 December 2008. http://www.nytimes.com/2008/12/13/business/13fraud.html. Retrieved on 15 December 2008.
* "Madoff Ran Vast Options Game". The Wall Street Journal. http://online.wsj.com/article/SB122938212422208613.html. Retrieved on 15 December 2008.
* "www.opednews.com/author/author2556.html". http://www.opednews.com/author/author2556.html.
* "www.opednews.com/articles/Re-Investing-With-Bernie-by-Lawrence-Velvel-090119-999.html". http://www.opednews.com/articles/Re-Investing-With-Bernie-by-Lawrence-Velvel-090119-999.html.

* "Madoff Scheme Kept Rippling Outward, Across Borders". The New York Times. 20 December 2008. http://www.nytimes.com/2008/12/20/business/20madoff.html?pagewanted=1&_r=1&em. Retrieved on 22 December 2008.

*
"www.nytimes.com/2008/12/13/nyregion/13madoff.html?

_r=2&ref=nyregion".
http://www.nytimes.com/2008/12/13/nyregion/13madoff.html?_r=2&ref=nyregion.

* "money.cnn.com/2008/12/29/news/newsmakers/zuckoff_madoff.fortune/".
http://money.cnn.com/2008/12/29/news/newsmakers/zuckoff_madoff.fortune/.

* "online.wsj.com/article/SB122910977401502369.html".
http://online.wsj.com/article/SB122910977401502369.html.

* The End of the Financial World as We Know It New York Times

* "www.tavakolistructuredfinance.com/TSF11.html".
http://www.tavakolistructuredfinance.com/TSF11.html.

* "Investor Furor Over '50B Scam'". New York Post. 14 December 2008.
http://m.nypost.com/ms/p/nyp/nyp/view.m?id=23907&storyid=143966. Retrieved on 17 December 2008.

* Biggs, Barton (12 January 2009). "The Affinity Ponzi Scheme". Newsweek CLIII (2): 39.

* "www.c-spanarchives.org/library/includes/templates/library/flash_

popup.php?pID=283836-1&clipStart=&clipStop=".
http://www.c-spanarchives.org/library/includes/templates/library/flash_popup.php?pID=283836-1&clipStart=&clipStop=.

* Schwartz, Nelson D. (24 December 2008). "Madoff Dealings Tarnish a Private Swiss Bank". The New York Times.
http://www.nytimes.com/2008/12/24/business/worldbusiness/24ubp.html?em. Retrieved on 23 December 2008.

* "Prominent Trader Accused of Defrauding Clients", [[The New York Times December 12, 2008]
* Sender, Henry (21 December 2008). "Madoff had 'perceived edge' in the markets". Financial Times.
http://www.ft.com/cms/s/0/534b1998-cf92-11dd-abf9-000077b07658,dwp_uuid=b7a8d610-caaf-11dd-87d7-000077b07658.html?nclick_check=1. Retrieved on 25 December 2008.

* "www.c-spanarchives.org/library/includes/templates/library/flash_popup.php?pID=283836-1&searchphrase=%20annual%20returns". http://www.c-spanarchives.org/library/includes/templates/library/flash_popup.php?pID=283836-1&searchphrase=%20annual%20returns.

* Scannell, Cara (5 January 2009). "Madoff Chasers Dug for Years, to No Avail". The Wall Street Journal.

http://online.wsj.com/article/SB123111743915052731.html?mod=googlenews_wsj. Retrieved on 5 January 2009.

* Carney, John (20 December 2008). "How Long Has This Been Going On?". Clusterstock (AlleyInsider). http://clusterstock.alleyinsider.com/2008/12/how-long-has-this-been-going-on. Retrieved on 25 December 2008.

* Norman, Bob (17 December 2008). "Fort Lauderdale Philanthropist Tied To Epic Swindler Madoff". Broward-Palm Beach New Times. http://blogs.browardpalmbeach.com/pulp/2008/12/michael_bienes_tied_to_bernard_madoff.php. Retrieved on 25 December 2008.

* "www.ack.net/avellino020309.html". http://www.ack.net/avellino020309.html.

* Healy (13 December 2008). "Boston donors bilked out of millions". Boston Globe. http://www.boston.com/business/articles/2008/12/13/boston_donors_bilked_out_of_millions/.

* "www.c-spanarchives.org/library/includes/templates/library/flash_popup.php?pID=283836-1&clipStart=&clipStop=". http://www.c-spanarchives.org/library/includes/templates/library/flash_popup.php?pID=283836-1&clipStart=&clipStop=.

* "online.wsj.com/article/SB123111743915052731.html?mod=googlenews_wsj". http://online.wsj.com/article/SB123111743915052731.html?mod=googlenews_wsj.

* "www.independent.co.uk/news/business/analysis-and-features/the-madoff-files-the-man-behind-the-most-audacious-fraud-in-history-1518939.html". http://www.independent.co.uk/news/business/analysis-and-features/the-madoff-files-the-man-behind-the-most-audacious-fraud-in-history-1518939.html.

* "www.c-spanarchives.org/library/includes/templates/library/flash_popup.php?pID=283836-1&clipStart=&clipStop=". http://www.c-spanarchives.org/library/includes/templates/library/flash_popup.php?pID=283836-1&clipStart=&clipStop=.

* "online.wsj.com/public/resources/documents/MarkopolosTestimony20090203.pdf" (PDF). http://online.wsj.com/public/resources/documents/MarkopolosTestimony20090203.pdf.

* "www.reuters.com/article/governmentFilingsNews/idUSN0245716120090202".

http://www.reuters.com/article/governmentFilingsNews/idUSN0245716120090202.

*
"www.bostonherald.com/business/general/view/2009_02_03_Man_who_warned_about_Bernard_Madoff_to_testify/srvc=business&position=also".
http://www.bostonherald.com/business/general/view/2009_02_03_Man_who_warned_about_Bernard_Madoff_to_testify/srvc=business&position=also.

* Madoff fraud case raises questions about SEC
Associated Press.

*
"www.bostonherald.com/business/general/view/2009_02_03_Man_who_warned_about_Bernard_Madoff_to_testify/srvc=business&position=also".
http://www.bostonherald.com/business/general/view/2009_02_03_Man_who_warned_about_Bernard_Madoff_to_testify/srvc=business&position=also.

* Weil, Jonathan (26 December 2008). "Madoff exposes double standard for Ponzi schemes". Bloomberg News (Greater Fort Wayne Business Weekly).
http://www.fwdailynews.com/articles/2008/12/26/greater_fort_wayne/features/opinion/letters_to_the_editor/hid108593sect_34f8ccf755b92af298.txt.

* Serchuk, David (20 December 2008). "Love, Madoff And The SEC". Forbes. http://www.forbes.com/intelligentinvesting/2008/12/20/intelligent-investing-madoff-sec-fraud-panelDec22.html?partner=contextstory. Retrieved on 24 December 2008.

* Markopolos, Harry (November 7, 2005). "The World's Largest Hedge Fund is a Fraud" (PDF). Wall Street Journal Online. http://online.wsj.com/documents/Madoff_SECdocs_20081217.pdf. Retrieved on December 22, 2008.

* "www.time.com/time/business/article/0,8599,1877181,00.html". http://www.time.com/time/business/article/0,8599,1877181,00.html.

* "www.counterpunch.org/velvel01212009.html". http://www.counterpunch.org/velvel01212009.html.

* "www.bloomberg.com/apps/news?pid=20601109&sid=aG5kjYW2AR5A&refer=home". http://www.bloomberg.com/apps/news?pid=20601109&sid=aG5kjYW2AR5A&refer=home.

* Abkowitz, Alyssa (18 December 2008). "Madoff's auditor... does not audit?". Fortune (CNNMoney.com).

http://money.cnn.com/2008/12/17/news/companies/madoff.auditor.fortune. Retrieved on 18 December 2008.

* Voreacos, David (16 December 2008). "New York Prosecutor Drops Madoff Auditor Probe; Defers to U.S.". Bloomberg News. http://www.bloomberg.com/apps/news?pid=20601087&sid=aAeIQnSSpJRQ&refer=home. Retrieved on 24 December 2008.

* Fitzgerald, Jim (18 December 2008). "Madoff's financial empire audited by tiny firm: one guy". Associated Press (Seattle Times). http://seattletimes.nwsource.com/html/businesstechnology/2008533585_madoff18.html. Retrieved on 18 December 2008.

* Kouwe, Zachery (December 15, 2008). "A Look at Madoff Trading Records". Deal Book. New York Times. http://dealbook.blogs.nytimes.com/2008/12/15/a-look-at-madoffs-trading-records/. Retrieved on December 22, 2008.

* Hamilton. "Madoff's reliable returns aroused doubts". LA Times. http://www.latimes.com/business/investing/la-fi-madoff13-2008dec13,0,4756661.story. Retrieved on 13 December 2008.

* For Madoff investors, big returns trumped concerns Associated Press.

* Zuckerman. "Fees, Even Returns and Auditor All Raised Flags". The Wall Street Journal. http://online.wsj.com/article/SB122910977401502369.html?mod=googlenews_wsj.

* E&P Staff (2009-02-04). "Whistleblower Claims He Tipped 'WSJ' to Madoff Fraud, Paper Failed to Act". http://www.editorandpublisher.com/eandp/news/article_display.jsp?vnu_content_id=1003938136.

* Friedman. "Charity Caught Up in Wall Street Ponzi Scandal". Fox News. http://www.foxnews.com/story/0,2933,466665,00.html. Retrieved on 13 December 2008.

* "www.bloomberg.com/apps/news?pid=20601103&sid=auW0pQ3I8lFo&refer=us". http://www.bloomberg.com/apps/news?pid=20601103&sid=auW0pQ3I8lFo&refer=us.

* "Madoff Sought, Got Cash in Days Before Arrest". SmartMoney. 2009-01-09. http://www.smartmoney.com/breaking-news/smw/?story=20090107105536. Retrieved on 2009-01-29.

* Berenson, Alex; Diana B. Henriques (15 December 2008). "Inquiry Finds No Signs Family Aided Madoff".

The New York Times. http://www.nytimes.com/2008/12/16/business/16madoff.html?em. Retrieved on 16 December 2008.

* Glovin, David (19 December 2008). "Madoff Restricted to Home; U.S. Warns of Harm, Flight". Bloomberg.com. http://www.bloomberg.com/apps/news?pid=20601087&sid=accRgQ_2s29o&refer=home. Retrieved on 21 December 2008.

* Neumeister, Larry (December 11, 2008). "Ex-Nasdaq chair arrested on fraud charge". Associated Press. http://biz.yahoo.com/ap/081211/wall_street_arrest.html. Retrieved on December 11, 2008.

* "Top Broker Accused of Fraud; Madoff, Money Manager for the Wealthy, Said to Have Run '$50 Billion Ponzi Scheme'". The Wall Street Journal. 11 December 2008. http://online.wsj.com/article/SB122903010173099377.html?mod=googlenews_wsj. Retrieved on 11 December 2008.

* "www.independent.co.uk/news/business/analysis-and-features/the-madoff-files-the-man-behind-the-most-audacious-fraud-in-history-1518939.html". http://www.independent.co.uk/news/business/analysis-and-features/the-madoff-files-the-man-behind-the-most-audacious-fraud-in-history-1518939.html.

* Henriques, Diana; Zachery Kouwe (11 December 2008). "Prominent Trader Accused of Defrauding Clients". The New York Times. http://www.nytimes.com/2008/12/12/business/12scheme.html?ref=business. Retrieved on 11 December 2008.

* Efrati, Amir; Aaron Lucchetti and Tom Lauricella (23 December 2008). "Probe Eyes Audit Files, Role of Aide To Madoff". The Wall Street Journal (Dow Jones). http://online.wsj.com/article/SB122999256957528605.html?mod=googlenews_wsj. Retrieved on 23 December 2008.

* "online.wsj.com/article/SB123384533479552435.html?mod=googlenews_wsj". http://online.wsj.com/article/SB123384533479552435.html?mod=googlenews_wsj.

* http://www.sec.gov/news/press/2008/2008-293-order-2.pdf SIPC page 7, VII United States Securities and Exchange Commission.

* Rush, George; Thomas Zambito, Phyllis Furman and Greg B. Smith (18 December 2008). "Bernard Madoff housebound after failing to get enough co-signers for bail bond in $50B ponzi scheme". New York Daily News. http://www.nydailynews.com/news/ny_crime/2008/12/17/2008-12-

17_bernard_madoff_housebound_after_failing_.html. Retrieved on 26 December 2008.

* Zambito, Thomas; Corky Siemaszko (20 December 2008). "Feds confine Bernie Madoff to his $7 million penthouse until trial". New York Daily News. http://www.nydailynews.com/news/ny_crime/2008/12/20/2008-12-20_feds_confine_bernie_madoff_to_his_7_mill.html. Retrieved on 26 December 2008.

* Glovin, David (6 January 2009). "Madoff Sons Reported Jewelry Violations to U.S., Lawyer Says". Bloomberg.com. http://www.bloomberg.com/apps/news?pid=20601103&sid=aRLjsVfmRQ64&refer=us. Retrieved on 6 January 2009.

* Berenson, Alex (6 January 2009). "Bid to Revoke Madoff's Bail Cites His Gifts". The New York Times. http://www.nytimes.com/2009/01/06/business/06madoff.html?em. Retrieved on 6 January 2009.

* Henrique, Diana (12 January 2009). "Judge Rules Madoff Can Remain Free on Bail". The New York Times. http://www.nytimes.com/2009/01/13/business/13bail.html?_r=1. Retrieved on 12 January 2009.

*
http://www.bloomberg.com/apps/news?pid=20601087&sid=aFZ1aoCd6BnQ&refer=home

*
http://money.cnn.com/2009/02/09/news/newsmakers/madoff_judgment/?postversion=2009020913

* http://blogs.wsj.com/law/2009/02/09/madoff-makes-peace-with-the-sec-amount-of-fine-tbd/

*
"online.wsj.com/article/SB123249539137500157.html?mod=googlenews_wsj".
http://online.wsj.com/article/SB123249539137500157.html?mod=googlenews_wsj.

* Madoff's Auditor CNN December 17, 2008.

* Bray, Chad (16 December 2008). "3rd UPDATE: Merkin, Ascot Fund Sued Over Madoff Investments". CNN (Dow Jones Newswires).
http://money.cnn.com/news/newsfeeds/articles/djf500/200812162136DOWJONESDJONLINE000783_FORTUNE5.htm. Retrieved on 23 December 2008.

* "Letter from Merkin to Investors" (PDF). The New York Times. 11 December 2008.
http://www.nytimes.com/packages/pdf/business/20081216_MERKIN.pdf. Retrieved on 19 December 2008.

* "Blumenthal May Investigate Charities Ripped Off By Madoff". Forbes. 22 December 2008. http://www.forbes.com/wallstreet/2008/12/22/madoff-blumenthal-charities-biz-wall-cz_cc_1222charities.html?partner=contextstory. Retrieved on 24 December 2008.

* ""Cuomo Issues Subpoenas Against Three Investment Funds Run by Merkin", Financial Times, 16 January 2009". http://www.ft.com/cms/s/0/51a152ac-e31e-11dd-a5cf-0000779fd2ac.html.

* "online.wsj.com/article/SB123189380284379481.html?mod=googlenews_wsj". http://online.wsj.com/article/SB123189380284379481.html?mod=googlenews_wsj.

* ""Jaffe Tarnished as Feds Investigate Madoff", Palm Beach Post (December 20, 2008)". http://www.palmbeachpost.com/localnews/content/local_news/epaper/2008/12/20/a1a_jaffe_1221.html.

* "business.timesonline.co.uk/tol/business/industry_sectors/banking_and_finance/article5562935.ece". http://business.timesonline.co.uk/tol/business/industry_sectors/banking_and_finance/article5562935.ece.

* "news.muckety.com/2009/01/15/cohmad-securities-robert-jaffe-face-tough-questions-about-madoff-ties/10151". http://news.muckety.com/2009/01/15/cohmad-securities-robert-jaffe-face-tough-questions-about-madoff-ties/10151.

* ""William Galvin Sues Salesman Robert Jaffe -- Demands Testimony", Boston Herald (January 15, 2009)". http://www.bostonherald.com/business/general/view/2009_01_15_William_Galvin_sues_salesman_Robert_Jaffe:_Demands_testimony/srvc=business&position=recent_bullet.

* "Beth Healy, "Madoff Associate Jaffe Skips State Hearing", Boston Globe (January 14, 2009)". http://www.boston.com/business/articles/2009/01/14/a_madoff_ally_skips_his_hearing/.

* "Cohmad Securities at Muckety.com". http://www.muckety.com/Cohmad-Securities/5058711.muckety.

* "www.nydailynews.com/news/us_world/2008/12/26/2008-12-26_forrest_gump_eric_roth_screenwriter_sues.html". http://www.nydailynews.com/news/us_world/2008/12/26/2008-12-26_forrest_gump_eric_roth_screenwriter_sues.html.

* "www.latimes.com/news/printedition/front/la-fi-madoff-chais21-2008dec21,0,7052710.story". http://www.latimes.com/news/printedition/front/la-fi-madoff-chais21-2008dec21,0,7052710.story.

* "www.politickernj.com/max/26238/weinberg-loses-life-savings-ponzi-scheme". http://www.politickernj.com/max/26238/weinberg-loses-life-savings-ponzi-scheme.

* "www.nytimes.com/2009/01/18/nyregion/new-jersey/18weinbergnj.html". http://www.nytimes.com/2009/01/18/nyregion/new-jersey/18weinbergnj.html.

* Gandel. "Madoff Victims Look for Ways to Recover Their Money". Time Magazine. http://www.time.com/time/business/article/0,8599,1866689,00.html. Retrieved on 17 December 2008.

* Honan, Edith; Dan Wilchins (12 December 2008). "Former Nasdaq chair arrested over alleged £33 billion fraud". International Herald Tribune. http://www.iht.com/articles/reuters/2008/12/12/business/OUKBS-UK-MADOFF-ARREST.php. Retrieved on 12 December 2008.

* Dozens of Defrauded Investors in Madoff Case Retain Milberg LLP and Seeger Weiss LLP to Seek Recovery of

Losses Hundreds of Millions of Dollars at Issue Marketwatch.com

* "www.bloomberg.com/apps/news?pid=20601087&sid=ax319OmN67Pg&refer=home". http://www.bloomberg.com/apps/news?pid=20601087&sid=ax319OmN67Pg&refer=home.

* Kim. "Investors May Have to Surrender Gains". The Wall Street Journal. http://online.wsj.com/article/SB122930184908605505.html?mod=googlenews_wsj. Retrieved on 19 December 2008.

* Varchaver (19 December 2008). "Some people who got out of Bernard Madoff Investment Securities before it imploded may have to give back gains.". CNN. http://money.cnn.com/2008/12/19/news/madoff.legal.fortune/?postversion=2008121909. Retrieved on 19 December 2008.

* "Another LI law firm targets Bernard Madoff". Newsday (Cablevision). 17 December 2008. http://www.newsday.com/news/local/longisland/ny-bzscam1812281321dec18,0,3154947.story. Retrieved on 19 December 2008.

* Kim. "Investors May Have to Surrender Gains". The Wall Street Journal.

http://www.bloomberg.com/apps/news?pid=20601103&sid=aTED8jdhJ.oE&refer=us. Retrieved on December 19, 2008.

* "No |title= specified". http://www.bloomberg.com/apps/news?pid=20601103&sid=aTED8jdhJ.oE&refer=us.

* "www.google.com/hostednews/ap/article/ALeqM5jFshcA2-NrmBjqZp8jkMHqknzI5gD964VCSO9". http://www.google.com/hostednews/ap/article/ALeqM5jFshcA2-NrmBjqZp8jkMHqknzI5gD964VCSO9.

* "www.newsday.com/services/newspaper/printedition/friday/business/ny-bzbank3012412203jan30,0,7387984.story". http://www.newsday.com/services/newspaper/printedition/friday/business/ny-bzbank3012412203jan30,0,7387984.story.

* "www.newsday.com/business/ny-bzmado236009159jan23,0,819611.story". http://www.newsday.com/business/ny-bzmado236009159jan23,0,819611.story.

* "www.bloomberg.com/apps/news?pid=20601103&sid=auW0pQ3I8lFo&refer=us".

http://www.bloomberg.com/apps/news?pid=20601103&si d=auW0pQ3I8lFo&refer=us.

* "www.usatoday.com/money/industries/brokerage/2009-01-28-madoff-car-deal_N.htm". http://www.usatoday.com/money/industries/brokerage/20 09-01-28-madoff-car-deal_N.htm.

* "www.bloomberg.com/apps/news?pid=20601103&sid=au W0pQ3I8lFo&refer=us". http://www.bloomberg.com/apps/news?pid=20601103&si d=auW0pQ3I8lFo&refer=us.

* "www.bloomberg.com/apps/news?pid=20601213&sid=a6 JDlygKnj8k&refer=home". http://www.bloomberg.com/apps/news?pid=20601213&si d=a6JDlygKnj8k&refer=home.

* "www.reuters.com/article/companyNewsAndPR/idUSN22 5386392009012 2". http://www.reuters.com/article/companyNewsAndPR/idU SN225386392009012 2.

* Szep. "Madoff fraud could burn early pullouts". Reuters. http://www.reuters.com/article/hedgeFundsNews/idUSLN E4BE01120081217. Retrieved on 17 December 2008.

* Coolidge (12 December 2008). "Lessons For Madoff Investors From The Bayou Fund Ponzi Scheme". Forbes. http://www.forbes.com/home/2008/12/12/madoff-redemptions-bayou-biz-wallst-cz_cc_1212madoff.html. Retrieved on 17 December 2008.

* Szep. "Madoff fraud could burn early pullouts". Reuters. http://www.thejewishweek.com/viewArticle/c36_a14606/News/New_York.html. Retrieved on December 17, 2008.

* "No |title= specified". http://www.thejewishweek.com/viewArticle/c36_a14606/News/New_York.html.

* "abcnews.go.com/TheLaw/Business/story?id=6554322&page=1". http://abcnews.go.com/TheLaw/Business/story?id=6554322&page=1.

* "business.smh.com.au/business/madoffs-assets-to-be-kept-secret-20090101-78f7.html". http://business.smh.com.au/business/madoffs-assets-to-be-kept-secret-20090101-78f7.html.

* "online.wsj.com/public/resources/documents/madoffclientlist020409.pdf" (PDF). http://online.wsj.com/public/resources/documents/madoffclientlist020409.pdf.

*
"www.time.com/time/business/article/0,8599,1877414,00.html".
http://www.time.com/time/business/article/0,8599,1877414,00.html.

*
"online.wsj.com/article/SB123384533479552435.html?mod=googlenews_wsj".
http://online.wsj.com/article/SB123384533479552435.html?mod=googlenews_wsj.

*
"www.foxbusiness.com/story/markets/industries/finance/madoffs-customer-list-reveals-thousands-names/".
http://www.foxbusiness.com/story/markets/industries/finance/madoffs-customer-list-reveals-thousands-names/.

* "Banks face huge losses from $50B ‘scam’". CNN. 15 December 2008.
http://www.cnn.com/2008/BUSINESS/12/15/madoff.arrest.exposure/index.html.

* Scheer, David; David Glovin (15 December 2008). "Madoff Said to Use Unregistered Side-Unit for Clients (Update5)". Bloomberg.com.
http://www.bloomberg.com/apps/news?pid=20601102&sid=aXWbLI1zC.Oo&refer=uk. Retrieved on 15 December 2008.

* ""Nadoff Client List Released", Associated Press via Yahoo News (February 5, 2009)". http://finance.yahoo.com/news/NY-court-document-reveals-apf-14260542.html.

* ""Gabor and Husband May Have Lost Money to Madoff", Associated Press via Yahoo News (January 25, 2009)". http://news.yahoo.com/s/ap/20090126/ap_en_ot/madoff_scandal_gabor.

* ""Zuckerman Sounds Off on Madoff", New York Daily News (December 14, 2008)". http://www.nypost.com/seven/12142008/news/regionalnews/daily_news_owner_mort_zuckerman_madoff_v_144237.htm.

* ""Gabor and Husband May Have Lost Money to Madoff", Associated Press via Yahoo News (January 25, 2009)". http://www.reuters.com/article/newsOne/idUSTRE50K6BO20090122.

* "Madoff's Victims". The Wall Street Journal. 16 December 2008. http://s.wsj.net/public/resources/documents/st_madoff_victims_20081215.html. Retrieved on 17 December 2008.

* Statement on Aozora's Exposure to Madoff Securities Aozora Bank. Retrieved on December 16, 2008.

* ="PBP">Clough, Alexandra (12 January 2009). "Some Madoff victims also lost big in KL scam". Palm Beach Post. http://www.palmbeachpost.com/localnews/content/business/epaper/2009/01/12/a1f_cloughcol_0112.html. Retrieved on 27 January 2009.

* aMadoff's Investors Had About $36 Billion With Firm: Table, Bloomberg News, December 24, 2008.

* Top 10 Madoff Losers, Politonomist.com, December 24, 2008.

* ""UBS Sued by Oddo et Cie Over Alleged Madoff Connection", Swissinfo.ch website (January 15, 2009)". http://ubs-news.newslib.com/story/7064-20075/.

* ""French Prosecutors Open Investigation of Madoff", Reuters via Yahoo News (January 20, 2009)". http://news.yahoo.com/s/nm/20090120/ts_nm/us_france_madoff;_ylt=AmL7JUJu0inJEvaigUn9t3J34T0D.

* ""Hegde Fund Loses Over $350 Million in Madoff Affair", Associated Press via Yahoo News (January 21, 2009)". http://news.yahoo.com/s/ap/20090121/ap_on_bi_ge/eu_switzerland_auriga_madoff.

* Some groups lower loss estimates in Madoff scandal, Associated Press, January 3, 2009.

* "Madoff Investor's Suicide Leaves Questions" by Alex Berenson and Matthew Saltmarsh, The New York Times, January 2, 2009, p. B1 New York edition

* "Police: Madoff Investor Found Dead of Suicide" (text and audio). AP Newswire. 1010 WINS. http://www.1010wins.com/pages/3547010.php. Retrieved on December 23, 2008.

* "Bernie Madoff should rot with rats, victim's pal says". New York Daily News. 25 December 2008. http://www.nydailynews.com/money/2008/12/25/2008-12-25_bernie_madoff_should_rot_with_rats_victi.html. Retrieved on 26 December 2008.

* "online.wsj.com/article/SB123361899636241467.html?mod=googlenews_wsj". http://online.wsj.com/article/SB123361899636241467.html?mod=googlenews_wsj.

* "www.bloomberg.com/apps/news?pid=20601103&sid=a8Pw8wT2dhH4&refer=us". http://www.bloomberg.com/apps/news?pid=20601103&sid=a8Pw8wT2dhH4&refer=us.

* NYCC Board of directors New York City Center.

* Moore. "Deal Journal Q&A: A Jewish Charity That Avoided Madoff". The Wall Street Journal. http://blogs.wsj.com/deals/2008/12/24/deal-journal-qa-a-jewish-charity-that-avoided-madoff/. Retrieved on 24 December 2008.

* "www.newsmeat.com/fec/bystate_detail.php?last=Madoff&first=Bernard". http://www.newsmeat.com/fec/bystate_detail.php?last=Madoff&first=Bernard.

GNU Free Documentation License

1. APPLICABILITY AND DEFINITIONS

This License applies to any manual or other work, in any medium, that contains a notice placed by the copyright holder saying it can be distributed under the terms of this License. Such a notice grants a world-wide, royalty-free license, unlimited in duration, to use that work under the conditions stated herein. The "Document", below, refers to any such manual or work. Any member of the public is a licensee, and is addressed as "you". You accept the license if you copy, modify or distribute the work in a way requiring permission under copyright law.

A "Modified Version" of the Document means any work containing the Document or a portion of it, either copied verbatim, or with modifications and/or translated into another language.

A "Secondary Section" is a named appendix or a front-matter section of the Document that deals exclusively with the relationship of the publishers or authors of the Document to the Document's overall subject (or to related matters) and contains nothing that could fall directly within that overall subject. (Thus, if the Document is in part a textbook of mathematics, a Secondary Section may not explain any mathematics.) The relationship could be a matter of historical connection with the subject or with related matters, or of legal, commercial, philosophical, ethical or political position regarding them.

The "Invariant Sections" are certain Secondary Sections whose titles are designated, as being those of Invariant Sections, in the notice that says that the Document is released under this License. If a section does not fit the above definition of Secondary then it is not allowed to be designated as Invariant. The Document may contain zero Invariant Sections. If the Document does not identify any Invariant Sections then there are none.

The "Cover Texts" are certain short passages of text that are listed, as Front-Cover Texts or Back-Cover Texts, in the notice that says that the Document is released under this License. A Front-Cover Text may be at most 5 words, and a Back-Cover Text may be at most 25 words.

A "Transparent" copy of the Document means a machine-readable copy, represented in a format whose specification is available to the general public, that is suitable for revising the document straightforwardly with generic text editors or (for images composed of pixels) generic paint programs or (for drawings) some widely available drawing editor, and that is suitable for input to text formatters or for automatic translation to a variety of formats suitable for input to text formatters. A copy made in an otherwise Transparent file format whose markup, or absence of markup, has been arranged to thwart or discourage subsequent modification by readers is not Transparent. An image format is not Transparent if used for any substantial amount of text. A copy that is not "Transparent" is called "Opaque".

Examples of suitable formats for Transparent copies include plain ASCII without markup, Texinfo input format, LaTeX input format, SGML or XML using a publicly available DTD, and standard-conforming simple HTML, PostScript or PDF designed for human modification. Examples of transparent image formats include PNG, XCF and JPG. Opaque formats include proprietary formats that can be read and edited only by proprietary word processors, SGML or XML for which the DTD and/or processing tools are not generally available, and the machine-generated HTML, PostScript or PDF produced by some word processors for output purposes only.

The "Title Page" means, for a printed book, the title page itself, plus such following pages as are needed to hold, legibly, the material this License requires to appear in the title page. For works in formats which do not have any title page as such, "Title Page" means the text near the most prominent appearance of the work's title, preceding the beginning of the body of the text.

A section "Entitled XYZ" means a named subunit of the Document whose title either is precisely XYZ or contains XYZ in parentheses following text that translates XYZ in another language. (Here XYZ stands for a specific section name mentioned below, such as "Acknowledgements", "Dedications", "Endorsements", or "History".) To "Preserve the Title" of such a section when you modify the Document means that it remains a section "Entitled XYZ" according to this definition.

The Document may include Warranty Disclaimers next to the notice which states that this License applies to the Document. These Warranty Disclaimers are considered to be included by reference in this License, but only as regards disclaiming warranties: any other implication that these Warranty Disclaimers may have is void and has no effect on the meaning of this License.

2. VERBATIM COPYING

You may copy and distribute the Document in any medium, either commercially or noncommercially, provided that this License, the copyright notices, and the license notice saying this License applies to the Document are reproduced in all copies, and that you add no other conditions whatsoever to those of this License. You may not use technical measures to obstruct or control the reading or further copying of the copies you make or distribute. However, you may accept compensation in exchange for copies. If you distribute a large enough number of copies you must also follow the conditions in section 3.

You may also lend copies, under the same conditions stated above, and you may publicly display copies.

3. COPYING IN QUANTITY

If you publish printed copies (or copies in media that commonly have printed covers) of the Document, numbering more than 100, and the Document's license notice requires Cover Texts, you must enclose the copies in covers that carry, clearly and legibly, all these Cover Texts: Front-Cover Texts on the front cover, and Back-Cover Texts on the back cover. Both covers must also clearly and legibly identify you as the publisher of these copies. The front cover must present the full title with all words of the title equally prominent and visible. You may add other material on the covers in addition. Copying with changes limited to the covers, as long as they preserve the title of the Document and satisfy these conditions, can be treated as verbatim copying in other respects.

If the required texts for either cover are too voluminous to fit legibly, you should put the first ones listed (as many as fit reasonably) on the actual cover, and continue the rest onto adjacent pages.

If you publish or distribute Opaque copies of the Document numbering more than 100, you must either include a machine-readable Transparent copy along with each Opaque copy, or state in or with each Opaque copy a computer-network location from which the general network-using public has access to download using public-standard network protocols a complete Transparent copy of the Document, free of added material. If you use the latter option, you must take reasonably prudent steps, when you begin distribution of Opaque copies in quantity, to ensure that this Transparent copy will remain thus accessible at the stated location until at least one year after the last time you distribute an Opaque copy (directly or through your agents or retailers) of that edition to the public.

It is requested, but not required, that you contact the authors of the Document well before redistributing any large number of copies, to give them a chance to provide you with an updated version of the Document.

4. MODIFICATIONS

You may copy and distribute a Modified Version of the Document under the conditions of sections 2 and 3 above, provided that you release the Modified Version under precisely this License, with the Modified Version filling the role of the Document, thus licensing distribution and modification of the Modified Version to whoever possesses a copy of it. In addition, you must do these things in the Modified Version:

* A. Use in the Title Page (and on the covers, if any) a title distinct from that of the Document, and from those of previous versions (which should, if there were any, be listed in the History section of the Document). You may use the same title as a previous version if the original publisher of that version gives permission.
* B. List on the Title Page, as authors, one or more persons or entities responsible for authorship of the modifications in the Modified Version, together with at least five of the principal authors of the Document (all of its principal authors, if it has fewer than five), unless they release you from this requirement.
* C. State on the Title page the name of the publisher of the Modified Version, as the publisher.
* D. Preserve all the copyright notices of the Document.

* E. Add an appropriate copyright notice for your modifications adjacent to the other copyright notices.
* F. Include, immediately after the copyright notices, a license notice giving the public permission to use the Modified Version under the terms of this License, in the form shown in the Addendum below.
* G. Preserve in that license notice the full lists of Invariant Sections and required Cover Texts given in the Document's license notice.
* H. Include an unaltered copy of this License.
* I. Preserve the section Entitled "History", Preserve its Title, and add to it an item stating at least the title, year, new authors, and publisher of the Modified Version as given on the Title Page. If there is no section Entitled "History" in the Document, create one stating the title, year, authors, and publisher of the Document as given on its Title Page, then add an item describing the Modified Version as stated in the previous sentence.
* J. Preserve the network location, if any, given in the Document for public access to a Transparent copy of the Document, and likewise the network locations given in the Document for previous versions it was based on. These may be placed in the "History" section. You may omit a network location for a work that was published at least four years before the Document itself, or if the original publisher of the version it refers to gives permission.
* K. For any section Entitled "Acknowledgements" or "Dedications", Preserve the Title of the section, and preserve in the section all the substance and tone of each of the contributor acknowledgements and/or dedications given therein.
* L. Preserve all the Invariant Sections of the Document, unaltered in their text and in their titles. Section numbers or the equivalent are not considered part of the section titles.
* M. Delete any section Entitled "Endorsements". Such a section may not be included in the Modified Version.
* N. Do not retitle any existing section to be Entitled "Endorsements" or to conflict in title with any Invariant Section.
* O. Preserve any Warranty Disclaimers.

If the Modified Version includes new front-matter sections or appendices that qualify as Secondary Sections and contain no material copied from the Document, you may at your option designate some or all of these sections as invariant. To do this, add their titles to the list of Invariant Sections in the

Modified Version's license notice. These titles must be distinct from any other section titles.

You may add a section Entitled "Endorsements", provided it contains nothing but endorsements of your Modified Version by various parties--for example, statements of peer review or that the text has been approved by an organization as the authoritative definition of a standard.

You may add a passage of up to five words as a Front-Cover Text, and a passage of up to 25 words as a Back-Cover Text, to the end of the list of Cover Texts in the Modified Version. Only one passage of Front-Cover Text and one of Back-Cover Text may be added by (or through arrangements made by) any one entity. If the Document already includes a cover text for the same cover, previously added by you or by arrangement made by the same entity you are acting on behalf of, you may not add another; but you may replace the old one, on explicit permission from the previous publisher that added the old one.

The author(s) and publisher(s) of the Document do not by this License give permission to use their names for publicity for or to assert or imply endorsement of any Modified Version.

5. COMBINING DOCUMENTS

You may combine the Document with other documents released under this License, under the terms defined in section 4 above for modified versions, provided that you include in the combination all of the Invariant Sections of all of the original documents, unmodified, and list them all as Invariant Sections of your combined work in its license notice, and that you preserve all their Warranty Disclaimers.

The combined work need only contain one copy of this License, and multiple identical Invariant Sections may be replaced with a single copy. If there are multiple Invariant Sections with the same name but different contents, make the title of each such section unique by adding at the end of it, in parentheses, the name of the original author or publisher of that section if known, or else a unique number. Make the same adjustment to the section titles in the list of Invariant Sections in the license notice of the combined work.

In the combination, you must combine any sections Entitled "History" in the various original documents, forming one section Entitled "History"; likewise combine any sections Entitled "Acknowledgements", and any sections Entitled "Dedications". You must delete all sections Entitled "Endorsements."

6. COLLECTIONS OF DOCUMENTS

You may make a collection consisting of the Document and other documents released under this License, and replace the individual copies of this License in the various documents with a single copy that is included in the collection, provided that you follow the rules of this License for verbatim copying of each of the documents in all other respects.

You may extract a single document from such a collection, and distribute it individually under this License, provided you insert a copy of this License into the extracted document, and follow this License in all other respects regarding verbatim copying of that document.

7. AGGREGATION WITH INDEPENDENT WORKS

A compilation of the Document or its derivatives with other separate and independent documents or works, in or on a volume of a storage or distribution medium, is called an "aggregate" if the copyright resulting from the compilation is not used to limit the legal rights of the compilation's users beyond what the individual works permit. When the Document is included in an aggregate, this License does not apply to the other works in the aggregate which are not themselves derivative works of the Document.

If the Cover Text requirement of section 3 is applicable to these copies of the Document, then if the Document is less than one half of the entire aggregate, the Document's Cover Texts may be placed on covers that bracket the Document within the aggregate, or the electronic equivalent of covers if the Document is in electronic form. Otherwise they must appear on printed covers that bracket the whole aggregate.

8. TRANSLATION

Translation is considered a kind of modification, so you may distribute translations of the Document under the terms of section 4. Replacing Invariant Sections with translations requires special permission from their copyright holders, but you may include translations of some or all Invariant Sections in addition to the original versions of these Invariant Sections. You may include a translation of this License, and all the license notices in the Document, and any Warranty Disclaimers, provided that you also include the original English version of this License and the original versions of those notices and disclaimers. In case of a disagreement between the translation and the original version of this License or a notice or disclaimer, the original version will prevail.

If a section in the Document is Entitled "Acknowledgements", "Dedications", or "History", the requirement (section 4) to Preserve its Title (section 1) will typically require changing the actual title.

9. TERMINATION

You may not copy, modify, sublicense, or distribute the Document except as expressly provided for under this License. Any other attempt to copy, modify, sublicense or distribute the Document is void, and will automatically terminate your rights under this License. However, parties who have received copies, or rights, from you under this License will not have their licenses terminated so long as such parties remain in full compliance.

10. FUTURE REVISIONS OF THIS LICENSE

The Free Software Foundation may publish new, revised versions of the GNU Free Documentation License from time to time. Such new versions will be similar in spirit to the present version, but may differ in detail to address new problems or concerns. See http://www.gnu.org/copyleft/.

Each version of the License is given a distinguishing version number. If the Document specifies that a particular numbered version of this License "or any later version" applies to it, you have the option of following the terms and conditions either of that specified version or of any later version that has been published (not as a draft) by the Free Software Foundation. If the Document does not specify a version number of this License, you may choose any version ever published (not as a draft) by the Free Software Foundation.

How to use this License for your documents

To use this License in a document you have written, include a copy of the License in the document and put the following copyright and license notices just after the title page:

Copyright (c) YEAR YOUR NAME.
Permission is granted to copy, distribute and/or modify this document under the terms of the GNU Free Documentation License, Version 1.2 or any later version published by the Free Software Foundation; with no Invariant Sections, no Front-Cover Texts, and no Back-Cover Texts. A copy of the license is included in the section entitled "GNU
Free Documentation License".

If you have Invariant Sections, Front-Cover Texts and Back-Cover Texts, replace the "with...Texts." line with this:

with the Invariant Sections being LIST THEIR TITLES, with the Front-Cover Texts being LIST, and with the Back-Cover Texts being LIST.

If you have Invariant Sections without Cover Texts, or some other combination of the three, merge those two alternatives to suit the situation.

If your document contains nontrivial examples of program code, we recommend releasing these examples in parallel under your choice of free software license, such as the GNU General Public License, to permit their use in free software.

4331809

Made in the USA
Lexington, KY
15 January 2010